D1385373

The Economics
of Global Trade

THE ECONOMICS OF GLOBAL TRADE

THE GLOBAL COMMUNITY:
    TECHNIQUES & STRATEGIES OF TRADE

THE GLOBAL ECONOMY AND THE ENVIRONMENT

GLOBAL INEQUALITIES AND THE FAIR TRADE
    MOVEMENT

GLOBAL TRADE IN THE ANCIENT WORLD

GLOBAL TRADE IN THE MODERN WORLD

GLOBAL TRADE ORGANIZATIONS

The Economics of Global Trade

Xina M. Uhl

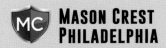

MASON CREST
PHILADELPHIA

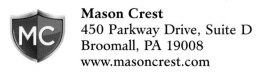

Mason Crest
450 Parkway Drive, Suite D
Broomall, PA 19008
www.masoncrest.com

Printed and bound in the United States of America.

CPSIA Compliance Information: Batch #CWI2016.
For further information, contact Mason Crest at 1-866-MCP-Book.

First printing
1 3 5 7 9 8 6 4 2

Library of Congress Cataloging-in-Publication Data

on file at the Library of Congress
ISBN: 978-1-4222-3663-5 (hc)
ISBN: 978-1-4222-8118-5 (ebook)

Understanding Global Trade and Commerce series ISBN: 978-1-4222-3662-8

Table of Contents

1: Economic Booms and Busts 7
2: Introduction to Economics 19
3: Supply and Demand.............................33
4: Money Management.............................45
5: National Economies
   and Globalization..............................57

Chronology 68
Organizations to Contact...........................71
Series Glossary 72
Further Reading 74
Internet Resources 75
Index 76
About the Author/Picture Credits................80

KEY ICONS TO LOOK FOR:

 Words to Understand: These words with their easy-to-understand definitions will increase the reader's understanding of the text, while building vocabulary skills.

 Sidebars: This boxed material within the main text allows readers to build knowledge, gain insights, explore possibilities, and broaden their perspectives by weaving together additional information to provide realistic and holistic perspectives.

 Research Projects: Readers are pointed toward areas of further inquiry connected to each chapter. Suggestions are provided for projects that encourage deeper research and analysis.

 Text-Dependent Questions: These questions send the reader back to the text for more careful attention to the evidence presented there.

 Series Glossary of Key Terms: This back-of-the book glossary contains terminology used throughout this series. Words found here increase the reader's ability to read and comprehend higher-level books and articles in this field.

Concerned people stand in the streets outside the New York Stock Exchange after the stock market experienced one of the largest single-day declines in its history, August 2011.

Economic Booms and Busts

Starting in 2006, Jennifer Butz struggled with health problems. She had a rare blood disorder. The Atlanta woman worked as a home loan officer. Her fragile health meant that she visited the hospital many times. This took its toll on her finances. She used credit cards to pay medical bills. In 2008 things got worse. She entered the hospital for more than a month. When she got out, she lost her job. She had taken out loans from banks to buy a house and a car. When she could not pay her house payment, the bank started a process to take it back. This is called *foreclosure*. She could not pay her car payment, either. The bank repossessed it.

In 2007, David Sutton lost his job. He had worked at the same company for 30 years. He was 54 years old. He looked for work every day at first, but he could not find a job. With no health insurance, his medical bills grew. His house lost value. His retirement savings dwindled. This difficult situation persisted for years. Then at 60 years of age Sutton had a heart attack and died. His family says that his money problems paid a role in his death.

Young people just out of college also suffered. Laura Sankey took out big loans to get through law school. In 2009 she graduated and began looking for work. Despite her qualifications she could not find a job. She had to move in with her grandfather. Her student loans totaled $100,000 but she had no work to pay them off. After many months of trying, she gave up on looking for legal work.

The stories of these people are not unique. They happened by the thousands all over North America and the world. Journalists began to call this economic downturn the Great Recession.

Boom and Bust

Economies like those in the US and Canada do not remain the same from year to year. They go through cycles. Boom times are when the economy grows. There are plenty of jobs. People who invest money in stocks and bonds earn good returns. Businesses make profits. Real

 Words to Understand in This Chapter

depression—a recession that lasts for an extended time and exceeds a recession in severity.

foreclosure—when borrowers cannot repay their loans, the lenders take back their property.

interest—an amount of money charged in order to borrow money.

recession—a bust cycle in the economy.

speculation—the use of borrowed funds in order to make risky investments in the hopes of receiving a large profit.

During "bust" periods in the economy, such as the Great Recession from 2007 to 2009, stores have a hard time making a profit and many will close their doors and go out of business.

estate value increases. Banks are happy to loan money to people. These times do not last forever, though.

Inevitably, the bust comes. The economy shrinks. There are fewer jobs. People who invest in stocks and bonds lose money. Many businesses close their doors. Others lay off workers and spend less. Real estate values decrease. Banks are reluctant to lend money to people. These bad times do not last forever, though, just like the boom times.

This cycle repeats regularly. Sometimes the boom times last longer and grow greater than others. Bust times can vary as well. Some last longer and are more severe than oth-

During the Great Recession that began in 2007, long-term unemployment figures reached record highs. In 2011, almost 33 percent of unemployed Americans had been without a job for 52 weeks. Fifteen percent had been unemployed for more than 99 weeks. African Americans and Asians suffered long-term unemployment at a higher rate than whites and Hispanics.

ers. A *recession* occurs when a bust lasts more than six months. Most times, a recession lasts from 6-18 months; six to ten percent of the workers are without jobs. A *depression* is a severe recession. This boom-bust cycle happened 11 times between 1945 and 2009.

The Housing Bubble Bursts

In the mid-1990s prices of houses began rising around 10 percent per year. The more they went up, the more people wanted to buy homes. Some worried that they would not be able to buy houses later if the price kept going up, so they hurried to buy themselves. Others hoped to buy houses and sell them again at a higher price to make big profits. This practice is called *speculation*. Because most people did not have enough money on hand to purchase a house, they went to banks to borrow money. Banks loaned money and charged *interest* to the borrower. Many lenders gave loans to people who might not be able to pay it back, hoping to make more from interest themselves.

The boom times lasted for a decade. The highest prices happened in 2006. Then in 2007, prices fell sharply. No

The housing bubble burst in 2007. Banks had extended credit, in the form of home mortgages, to many people who were barely able to afford the payments. To avoid high payments, many borrowers took out adjustable-rate mortgages. These had a lower initial interest rate. But as the low introductory-rate mortgages reverted to regular interest rates, borrowers were unable to pay. They defaulted on the loans.

more new houses were being built. Housing businesses laid off workers. Home sales fell. Many businesses closed shop. Interest rates increased. Rising numbers of people could not pay their home loans. As a result, banks began to foreclose on homes. Banks lost money because they had loaned out more money than the homes were worth now.

A Gloomy Past

For a while, many feared that a depression would happen. In the 1930s the Great Depression caused chaos in the United States. The stock market crashed, resulting in the loss of millions of dollars. Banks failed, wiping out the savings of many people. Unemployment surged. People lost their homes at a much greater rate than normal. Many people went hungry. This bust continued from 1929 to 1940. Before long, the Great Depression expanded to Canada, and then around the world.

The United States learned valuable lessons from the Great Depression. Laws made banks stronger and safer. Government policies kept such a big calamity from happening again. They could not prevent it entirely, though. Nothing could.

The Great Recession

In 2007, some protections kept the economy from reaching the depths suffered during the Great Depression. However, times were still hard. Banks had difficulties, and some failed. In 2009 a total of 176 banks closed their doors. Banks that held on slowed making loans to a trickle. The stock market dropped. At the lowest point, stocks fell 54 percent from the market high in October 2007. Businesses slowed their operations or closed. Unemployment grew to 10.2 percent, the highest it had been in about twenty years. This period became known as the Great Recession. It lasted from December 2007 to June 2009.

The US government took many measures to halt the damage from the recession. It helped keep interest rates

The period of economic hard times known as the Great Depression lasted for about eleven years. The US economy did not start to grow again until the late 1930s. This was because the start of the Second World War increased the global demand for American manufacturing and agricultural products to a greater level than ever before.

low, and loaned banks and large corporations money to keep them from closing. In turn for lending money the government owned parts of the banks and companies. In 2009, it owned about 80 percent of American International Insurance Group (AIG) and 60 percent of General Motors. It also owned part of about 700 banks. All together, it loaned out $4 trillion. These loans were paid back in a speedy manner most of the time, but still the government lost about $1.2 trillion. But most people agreed this was a good trade for preventing a complete economic collapse.

The Struggle of the Unemployed

As the Great Recession dragged on, many workers drew unemployment benefits. Unemployment compensation is money that states provide to people who are out of work. It helps them to survive until they can find a new source of income. In normal times, unemployed people can stay on these benefits for no more than about six months. During the Great Recession, though, benefits were extended to 99 weeks, or nearly two years. In Canada a similar system of benefits exists. It is called Employment Insurance. Employers and employees both pay amounts called premiums to fund this program.

While the economy in Canada experienced a downturn from late 2008 through about mid-2009, it was not as deep or lasting as in the United States. In Canada, the recession was mild. The highest unemployment rate suffered was 8.7 percent in August 2009. The exporting of automobiles, mostly to the US, declined sharply. However, problems with

Protesters gather in a park in New York City to demonstrate against the government's economic policies, as well as social and economic inequality. The Occupy Wall Street movement began in the fall of 2011, and soon spawned protests in other cities around the world.

Government Aid during the Recession

The United States Treasury department created a group of programs to slow the damage from the Great Recession. These were known as the Troubled Asset Relief Program (TARP). At first, Congress approved a 2008 bill for $700 billion. Later, the Dodd-Frank Wall Street Reform and Consumer Protection Act (Dodd-Frank Act) reduced that figure to $475 billion. Approximate amounts were committed as follows:

- $250 billion to assist banks ($5 billion was later cancelled).
- $27 billion to restart credit markets.
- $82 billion to assist the U.S. auto industry ($2 billion was later cancelled).
- $70 billion to assist American International Group (AIG) ($2 billion was later cancelled).
- $46 billion to assist families avoid foreclosure.

The American Recovery and Reinvestment Act of 2009 also helped. Barack Obama signed it into law less than a month after taking office as president, on February 17, 2009. It included a number of proposals such as tax credits, construction projects, health care initiatives, and education funding. Of these, $150 billion assisted individuals directly.

To combat the recession in Canada, the Bank of Canada acted several times to reduce interest rates for loans. Canada also cut business tax rates to 16.5 percent. This cut made Canada an attractive place for businesses to operate in.

credit and loans did not affect Canadian banking as severely as in the US. In 2010, the economy moved toward a quick recovery.

An Upward Turn

Recovery in the US has been much slower and weaker. Of the recessions since 1960, it has taken the longest and the economy has grown the least. Six years later, the economy improved, but not quickly or easily. In a recent poll by the Pew Research Center, only 6 percent of people described their financial recovery as excellent. The rest described it as fair, good, or poor.

 ## Text-Dependent Questions

1. Problems in which market started the Great Recession?
2. In what ways did the government try to limit the impact of the Great Recession?

 ## Research Project

For your research project, research the average income of residents or unemployment figures in your home state or province from the years 2005-2015. Have a librarian, teacher, or parent assist you in locating websites or books with this information. Then create a graph to show how the Great Recession affected your home state or province. The vertical axis should show the years 2005-2015. The horizontal axis should show either the average income of residents or unemployment figures. For each figure, draw an imaginary line to the right from the date and up from the horizontal axis. At the point in which these two lines meet, draw a dot. Do this for each yearly figure. Then connect the dots in an unbroken line. The line you create will show a trend. Discuss the trend you find in a written paragraph, being sure to use figures from the graph.

Today, countries like the United States and Canada are involved in a global economy, in which products are manufactured and shipped to consumers all over the world.

Introduction to Economics

The study of economics starts with a challenging idea. Human beings cannot have everything they want. Sometimes, we cannot even have everything we need. *Needs* are things that are necessary for survival, such as food, water, and shelter. *Wants* are things that are not absolutely necessary but that make life more pleasant, such as video games, jewelry, and artwork.

People meet their needs and fulfill their wants by acquiring goods and services. *Goods* are items that are for sale, like furniture, purses, or dinner plates. *Services* are actions that people perform for each other. Examples are haircuts, postal deliveries, and dental work.

Many people desire to purchase a greater amount of goods and services than they have the money or **resources** to acquire. They are limited by the funds that they have available. Even people with a lot of money face limits, as there is not an endless supply of goods that can be purchased. Both rich and poor face another limit: time. There are only 24 hours in a day, which limits the amount of time a person can work to earn more money, or *capital*. When something is in short supply, such as time, money, or goods, this is known as *scarcity*.

Scarcity is the basis of economics. It forces people to make choices about how to use resources like money and time. People must decide how to use their resources in a way that satisfies their basic needs. Excess resources can be used to satisfy their wants through the purchase of extra goods and services. Economics is the study of how people choose to satisfy their wants and needs.

Opportunities and Costs

When people make choices they must deal with trade-offs. In order to obtain something they need or want, they often

 Words to Understand in This Chapter

bureaucracy—government officials and the complicated process they use to perform tasks.

capital—wealth in the form of money or other assets owned by a person or organization or available or contributed for a particular purpose such as starting a company or investing.

opportunity cost—the loss of potential gain from other alternatives when one alternative is chosen.

resources—the supply of money, products, or energy.

scarcity—a limited amount of goods and services to meet unlimited desires.

Economics is about the decisions that people make with their money or resources. For example, if a person decides to purchase a non-essential item (such as a fishing rod), he will have less money to spend on other items.

have to give up something else. For example, when young people go to school they give up the freedom to play all day long in exchange for the opportunity to gain an education. When a business decides to close for a day, the owners gain a day off of work, but they lose the income they might have made from sales that day. One decision can have many trade-offs. One of these trade-offs is usually harder to give up than others. This is called the *opportunity cost*.

For example, a woman must determine whether she wants to take a bus to the grocery store. If she takes the bus she has to pay a bus fare of $1.00. She will get to the store faster than if she walks. Paying the fare will mean that she cannot spend that dollar on a pack of gum, though. The opportunity cost in this case is the pack of gum.

Questions and Answers

Each person in a society must decide how to produce, buy, and use goods and services for themselves. Society as a whole also has decisions to make. There are three key economic questions:

1. What goods and services should be produced? People must figure out whether it will be more efficient to build cars or make cheese to sell. Will they grow bananas, or mine copper?

2. How should these goods and services be produced? Not every country has the same resources, such as raw materials in the land. Labor, or workers, are those people who are not in the military and available to work. Labor can be found in all countries. Capital is also important. It can be invested into educating and training workers, or into purchasing equipment, buildings, and tools that workers can use to make products.

3. Who uses these goods and services? This question is about those who control the available money. The poor have little. The rich can buy fancy cars if they want. They can live in large

Chinese workers assemble clocks in a factory in the Shenzhen special economic zone. Laborers can be found in all countries.

homes by the ocean, where rents are high. Someone owns land. Do they collect rent from tenants? Do teachers earn more than lawyers?

The answers to these questions can be used to create ideas and rules by which a society manages the distribution of goods and services. This is known as an economic system.

Goats graze at the Bakara Animal Market in Mogadishu, Somalia. There are few countries today that only employ a traditional economy. However, some elements of the traditional economy, such as bartering and trading of goods and services, remain common in many rural areas of the developing world. The traditional economy is often characterized by subsistence farming, in which little surplus is produced.

Traditional Economies

A traditional economy is the oldest and least complicated kind of economy. Families form the basis of the workforce. Custom and habit are valued. People respect the ways that activities have been done by their ancestors. Oftentimes, men do different jobs than women. Women may cook and care for the children. Men may hunt and protect the family. Change is not encouraged.

One example of this system is found among the Inuit of Alaska and northern Canada. For thousands of years they have fished, hunted, and created shelters to survive. The cold weather makes life difficult. They share their food with the community. When they need items they cannot make themselves, they usually trade for them.

Command Economies

In a command economy, also called a centrally planned economy, decisions are made by a central governing power. Usually a dictator or a single political party runs things. A *bureaucracy* controlled by the leader carries out his or her wishes. The government decides what items will be produced, how they will be created, and who will get them. For example, the government may determine the number of pants, dishes, computers, and more that will be produced. They choose the color, size, quality, type, and price as well. Most of the time, socialist or communist countries have command economies.

Socialism values equality between people more than how

The father of communism was a German philosopher named Karl Marx (1818-1883). His book, The Communist Manifesto, *called for the end of capitalism and the start of a new society in which all of the workers would share ownership of the factories and means of production.*

In China, the Communist Party led by Mao Zedong created detailed plans for the national economy. This 1956 poster explains the party's ideas for the development of farming over the following decade. Unfortunately, central planning of the economies rarely worked as Communist leaders intended. In China, Mao's ambitious plans for economic growth—known as the Great Leap Forward—was a dismal failure. It resulted in a famine during the early 1960s that killed over 20 million Chinese.

much they can achieve. Workers are considered good depending on how much time they work. The things that the workers do is not as important. People depend on the government for basic services like food and medicine. Workers earn money and spend it as they like, although the government takes a significant share to fund its programs for the entire society. Today, countries like Brazil, Chile, and Venezuela are socialist.

Communism is more strict than socialism. In theory, the working class owns everything. No one is rich or poor; everyone is equal. If one person works longer hours at a harder job they do not get paid better than a person who works fewer hours at an easier job. Everyone works for the common good. Because people are not rewarded for their efforts, fewer goods are produced. The government limits people's freedom and expects complete obedience. In the past, the Soviet Union was communist. Today, North Korea, China, and Cuba are examples of communist countries.

Free Market Economy

The third type of economic system is a free market economy. It is also called free enterprise, or capitalism. In this system, citizens, not the government, own and run companies. Companies compete with each other to sell goods and services. Citizens decide on their own what to sell, where to sell it, and what prices to charge. They use their own money to start businesses with the hopes of making a profit. Citizens can also buy their own land, or private property.

According to economic theory, the free enterprise marketplace operates efficiently on its own, without the need for government regulation or interference. Adam Smith called this process "the invisible hand."

In 1776, Adam Smith published a book called *The Wealth of Nations.* He described the functions of a market. People, he said, only consider their own personal gain when buying and selling. This personal gain pushes people to look for lower prices. Businesses work to sell more goods. This increases their profits. Competition results when businesses who sell similar goods adjust their prices to gain more customers. For example, if two stores sell the same kind of milk, each will need to price it at about the same. Otherwise, consumers may not buy the milk that costs more.

The free market adjusts itself with little involvement by the government, an idea called *laissez faire.* Instead, competition and consumers' self-interest work together to keep it going.

The free market has many advantages. It regulates itself. It encourages growth. A greater variety of goods are available, giving consumers choices of what to buy. Many

 Did You Know?

Laissez faire, the belief that government should not interfere in the economy, is a French term. It means "let people do as they choose."

When the British owned Hong Kong from 1841 to 1997, they established a free market economy in the city. China, a communist country, controls Hong Kong today. However, banks in Hong Kong are still owned privately, and foreign trade occurs without the difficult economic barriers that communist and socialist government often erect.

countries practice capitalism today, like the United States, Canada, Germany, Great Britain, and Japan.

Mixed Economies

Each type of system has advantages and disadvantages. In a free market if the government does not participate, how will roads and bridges get built? Who will care for the poor? If people pay for the education of their children themselves then those who cannot afford it will be left out. In the United States and Canada, the government takes on these responsibilities. A mixed economy, then, involves some government regulation and oversight. However, government involvement is much more limited than in a command economy. Economic matters are not planned in a central fashion.

 Health Care in Canada and the US

Canada and the United States share more than a border. They are also alike economically. Both have free market systems. The health care systems between the countries differ, however. Canada's health-care system has more socialist elements.

In the United States, medical care is expensive. In fact, it is the most costly care in the world. Most workers have health insurance to cover all or part of their health care costs. The premiums are often paid by both the employer and the employee. Many people, however, do not have health insurance, making it difficult for them to afford medical care.

In 2010, the US Congress passed the Affordable Care Act. Its goal was to insure more people and lower costs. By 2016, many low-wage workers had been insured thanks to the Affordable Care Act. More than 10 percent of the uninsured still have no coverage, though.

Some of the poorest American citizens are insured by state programs. Those who are 65 or older or disabled people of all ages are covered by Medicare, which makes hospital stays and doctor visits free. It is paid for by the federal government.

In 1984 the Canada Health Care Act made medical care free for all citizens of Canada. It is similar to Medicare in the US. Almost all costs are covered except eyeglasses and dental care. Many people have extra insurance that covers these needs. The Canadian government bargains with drug companies to lower the cost of prescription drugs.

China, which has the world's largest economy, is officially a communist country. However, China's government has adopted some aspects of the free market system. It has allowed limited private ownership of businesses and farms. It has grown closer to a mixed economy in recent years.

 ## Text-Dependent Questions

1. What country in today's world has a mixed economy?
2. What is a key ingredient of a free market economy?
3. What are scarcity and opportunity cost? Why do they form the basis of economics?

 ## Research Project

Everyone wants something. Choose an item for purchase, such as a video game, book, or piece of jewelry. Research the price of the item in stores or online. Make a chart of the opportunity cost and trade-offs of spending money on the chosen item. Write a paragraph explaining what opportunity cost is and how you chose it for this assignment.

The law of supply and demand is a theory about the interaction between the amount of something that is available, the need for that item, and its price. If the supply of something is low and the demand is high, then the price will be high. If the supply of something is high and the demand is low, the price will be low.

3

Supply and Demand

Supply and demand are two basic economic ideas. While they usually interact with each other, they are different things. *Supply* is the amount of goods available. The law of supply says that as the price of a good rises the amount of goods, or the **quantity** available, will also rise. The price falls as the quantity of goods available falls.

Demand is when someone wants to own a good enough to pay for it. The law of demand says that the amount of a desirable good falls as the price rises. The opposite is also true.

For example, Fresh Time grocery store has 100 pounds of cherries for sale for $5.00 per pound. Their supply is 100. If 150 people come into the store wishing to buy one pound of cherries each, the demand for cherries is greater than the supply. According to the laws of supply and demand, the store will order more cherries to sell so that they can meet the demand.

The store will also raise the price of the cherries to increase their profit.

Assume that only 75 people come into the store wishing to buy one pound of cherries, not 150 people. In this case, the demand for cherries is less than the supply. The laws of supply and demand say that the store will lower the price of the cherries. As a result, the quantity will fall as more people buy them.

When the amount of a good demanded and the quantity supplied match each other the market reaches a stable point. This is known as *equilibrium*. Whenever these two do not match the market is not stable. This is called *disequilibrium*. It produces either a shortage or overage of goods. An overage is also called surplus.

Shortages result when the demand is greater than the supply as a result of low prices. A surplus occurs when the higher price reduces the amount demanded. This leaves leftovers from the quantity supplied. Both these conditions show disequilibrium. Equilibrium happens at a price point where demand equals supply.

 Words to Understand in This Chapter

debt—an amount due.

income—a gain from labor, business, or property.

quantity—an amount or number.

regulate—to bring under control.

Union and labor activists gathered along Varick Street in 2015 to urge the New York Wage Board to increase the city's minimum wage to $15 per hour. Workers have made similar requests in other American cities.

Balancing the Scale

Markets tend to balance out on their own. Sometimes the government interferes to set a price on a good or service. One example is rent control. In certain places the price of apartment or home rent is established by local laws. The price may be lower than the equilibrium price. It is a price ceiling—the highest price that can legally be charged for rent. This keeps prices low when rents are rising.

Government can also interfere in the other direction. They can set the lowest price for a good or service. This is called a price floor. The minimum wage for workers is one example of a price floor. The federal government requires states to pay workers no less than a certain amount. The current minimum wage is $7.25 per hour. States can require that workers be paid more than this amount, though.

In Canada, there is no one minimum wage for the whole country. Instead, the minimum wage depends on the province where the employee works. In 2016 this amount ranged from $10.30 per hour to $12.50 per hour. It is usually adjusted every year according to the Consumer Price Index. The Consumer Price Index compiles the ups and downs of prices for goods and services. It compares the costs of goods and services over time and finds a price in the middle.

Changes in Demand

Prices rise and fall due to many factors. One of these is elasticity of demand. The word *flexible* is a good synonym for elasticity. It means that the price increase on a good or service will cause some buyers to reduce their purchase of it. When the price decreases, then, some buyers will buy more of it.

When a consumer buys about the same amount of something after a large price increase, demand is said to be inelastic. If that consumer buys a lot less of something after a small price increase, their demand is said to be elastic.

Several factors affect elasticity. If there is a substitute for a good, buyers may choose it. If a certain brand of com-

In 2016, American and Canadian motorists benefitted from gasoline prices that fell to their lowest level in more than a decade. The price decline was due to overproduction of oil by countries like Saudi Arabia, Iran, Russia, and the United States. Because the supply of oil was greater than the demand, prices dropped. While good news for consumers, the low prices hurt the oil industry—many companies reduced or closed their operations, and an estimated 250,000 oil industry workers lost their jobs in 2016.

puter climbs in price, consumers may choose a different brand with a lower price. The importance of a good matters, too. If a worker needs to fuel his car to make it to work it is an important good. If the price of fuel rises, he may have to cut back on food or clothing to pay for gas. Necessities versus luxuries make a difference, too. Food is a necessity. A nicely decorated chocolate cake is a luxury. It

In 2015, the corporation Wal-Mart topped the list of the most wealthy companies in the world, with operating income at about 27 billion dollars. Currently, it runs more than 11,000 stores globally, with more than 5,200 in the United States and 400 in Canada.

likely costs more than a can of cooked beans. A buyer may then decide that the luxury costs too much.

Time affects elasticity, too. If the price of peanuts rises sharply, consumers may still purchase it for a while. They need time to find a substitute. The price remains inelastic. Over time consumers may substitute a lower cost item, such as sunflower seeds. This will cause the demand for peanuts to decrease. The price will then respond by becoming elastic.

Going to Market

The word *market* occurs a lot in economics. A market can be a local flower shop, a website where dog walkers offer their services, or a huge bank with offices all over the world. It is any place where buyers and sellers exchange goods or services. There, prices change as supply and demand changes. Competition causes businesses work against each other to earn consumers' business. Competition makes businesses produce more goods. It also keeps prices lower since consumers tend to choose the lower price items.

The simplest type of market is perfect competition, or pure competition. In it, many businesses produce the same product. Each competitor sells this product for the same price. No one business produces enough supply to change the price themselves. Products that are the same regardless of who produces them, are commodities. Examples are corn, paper, and gasoline.

 Did You Know?

A *cartel* is a group of companies that works together to form a monopoly on the production and sale of certain goods. Cartels are illegal in the United States, but in other areas such as Japan and Western Europe they are legal.

In 1973-1974 the US experienced a gasoline shortage. It resulted from members of a cartel called the Organization of Petroleum Exporting Countries (OPEC) refusing to sell oil to the US due to its support of Israel during the 1973 Arab-Israeli war. Such a refusal is called an *embargo*.

A business that tries to enter a market may encounter barriers to entry. A barrier keeps something from happening. A business may find it is very expensive to get the items and workers necessary to make and sell products. These are called start-up costs. Businesses that do not have enough money run up against a barrier that keeps them from entering the market.

Monopoly: Not Just a Game

At times, there is only one business providing a particular item or service. This is called a monopoly. Monopolies have no competition, so they can choose whatever price they want for goods or services. Barriers to entry keep other companies from entering this market. High prices can affect consumers because of this.

A natural monopoly runs most efficiently as the single provider of a good or service. Water service can be an example. A competitor would need to invest lots of money to set up pipes, pumping stations, and reservoirs. High start-up costs means they will have to charge a certain price to make money. But they must also keep costs low enough to compete. This can cause one or both water providers to go out of business. Since water is necessary for a town the government will sometimes take over a natural monopoly and *regulate* it to make sure it runs well.

The US has set up anti-trust laws to regulate monopolies. A trust is a number of firms who work together as one. The Sherman Anti-Trust Act of 1890 made trusts illegal. For many years, US telephone service was a monopoly. The company's name was American Telephone and Telegraph, or AT&T. AT&T controlled the cables and other networks that made phone calls possible. At first it was a natural monopoly. Then AT&T tried to control all long distance calls. In 1982 the government broke up AT&T into seven smaller companies.

Types of Businesses

Businesses have different types of organization. This

 A Tale of Two Monopolies

The most popular operating system on most computers is called Windows. It is made by the company Microsoft.

In 1999, the US Department of Justice sued Microsoft. It claimed that Microsoft was a monopoly. The reason why had to do with programs called web browsers, which people use to gain access to the internet. Microsoft included its own browser, Internet Explorer, with every copy of Windows that was sold. Browsers from competing companies, such as Netscape, did not run as well as they should have in the Windows operating system. A federal court ruled that Microsoft's practices stifled competition and made Microsoft a monopoly. They had to change their practices. Today, there are many rival web browsers, such as Google Chrome and Mozilla Firefox.

In 1981, legislation called the Canada Post Corporation Act created a monopoly. The Canada Post Corporation would handle Canadian mail delivery for letters weighing less than 500 grams. The system, known as Canada Post, has critics. Part of this involves postal employees, who are organized into a union. The union has called for strikes, or periods of no work, in the past. In June 2011 mail delivery throughout Canada was stopped. Critics of the Canada Post system claim that private companies could operate the postal system quicker and cheaper. For now, though, the Canada Post monopoly remains in effect.

Multinational corporations have manufacturing facilities and sell their products in several foreign countries. This Pepsi Corporation soda bottling plant is located in Samara, Russia.

depends on the size of a business, the number of people in it, profit, and taxes.

The simplest, easiest, most popular type of business is owned and run by one person. This is a sole proprietorship. It is usually small and local. Think about a nearby barber, café, or clothing shop. They are probably sole proprietorships. They are easy to start. They also receive all the profits themselves.

A partnership is owned by two or more people. They share the work and the profits. Partnerships are similar to sole proprietorships in many ways. They also have important differences. It is easier for them to get credit. Often partners take over different responsibilities in the business. This can make running the business easier because one person does not have to do everything. Firms that offer professional services, such as legal, accounting, or medical work, are often formed as partnerships.

A corporation is the most complex type of business. People who own stock, or certificates of ownership, technically own a small share of the business. Stockholders elect a board of directors to run the corporation. They also decide on officers to help run the corporation. The biggest advantage of a corporation is protection from liability. If a corporation loses money, individual stockholders are not required to pay back the *debt*. Corporations must pay taxes on their *income*, just like individuals. There are several different types of corporations.

 # Text-Dependent Questions

1. What is disequilibrium?
2. What are the three main types of business organizations?

 # Research Project

Research the minimum wage in your country or province for a fast-food cashier. Then call two fast-food restaurants in the closest community and ask for the manager at each location. Tell this person that you are working on a research project and you would like to know how much they pay employees per hour. Then write two paragraphs in which you define minimum wage from the text, list the results you found, and come up with reasons to justify your results.

The US dollar is the official currency of the United States. It is the currency most used in international transactions, and dollars are also held by the governments of many countries as a reserve currency.

4

Money Management

I t may seem strange, but money can be more than dollars and coins. Money took different forms throughout history. Sheep and cattle are the oldest forms of money. Salt, shells, and furs have also been used. Today's paper bills and coins are called *currency*. Money has six characteristics.

1. It must last when being handled.
2. It must be portable.
3. It must be easily divided. If a meal costs $5 and a person pays for it with a $10 bill they need to receive the remainder, or $5.
4. It must be the same in terms of what it will buy, or uniform. One large shell may buy a chicken, for example. Two small shells may buy an egg. One large shell would be worth more than two small shells.
5. It is in limited supply. Gold, for example, is relatively rare. The amount of it available in the world is set.

6. It must be acceptable. In North America, paper bills and coins are acceptable means of paying for purchases. Paying for a hotel room with shells or a sheep, however, would probably not be acceptable.

Banks

A bank is a place for receiving, storing, and loaning money. Customers can open checking and savings accounts. They can deposit their money in a checking account. It will allow them to withdraw the money or add more to it. A savings account is a place to deposit money for later use. Banks also issue debit and credit cards. A debit card can be used like cash at a store. It takes the purchase from the user's checking account. A credit card is used like a bank loan. The purchase is added to a balance. The bank charges interest on the balance until it is paid off.

A special kind of bank loan is a mortgage. It is used to buy property. Home mortgages are loans to purchase

 Words to Understand in This Chapter

budget—a plan for the use of money.

fixed income—a pre-set amount of money that people, such as retirees or the disabled, must live on each month.

investment—spending money in order to make a profit.

maturity—the date when a note becomes due.

quarter—a three-month period in a year.

This skyscraper houses the offices of the large investment banking firm Goldman Sachs. An investment bank is much different than a commercial bank. which is a place where people can deposit their money. An investment bank is a financial institution that helps wealthy individuals, corporations, and governments to raise money through issuing securi-

homes. An ***investment*** is a key part of free enterprise. It is the use of money to earn more money in the future. For instance, a man wishes to buy an antique car. He knows that the car will increase in value because it is in good shape and it is rare. When he sells the car later, he will likely make a profit. This is a good investment.

Bonds

A bond is a type of agreement between a government or corporation and an investor. The investor loans money to

A country's gross domestic product (GDP) is calculated using the following formula: Consumption + Government Expenditures + Investment + (Exports − Imports). GDP is a measure of the total economic activity within a country during a year.

these organizations. They promise to pay the investor back with interest over time. There are different kinds of bonds.

- Savings bonds. These are issued by the US government and used to raise money to pay for public projects such as roads, dams, and buildings. The investor has little risk because the government will not default, or become unable to pay back the loan plus interest.
- Treasury bonds are also issued by the US government. They are also called T-bills or T-notes. They can be used for different lengths of time. When this time is up it is known as *maturity*. Then the loan will be fully paid back, including interest.
- Municipal bonds are offered by state and local governments. They are used to build things like schools and libraries.
- Corporate bonds are offered by private businesses. They are riskier than those offered by governments. But it is possible to earn higher interest because of this risk.

Other types of investments are certificates of deposit (CDs) and money market mutual funds. Both are offered by banks. They use the depositor's money for a period of time such as a year. That money earns interest.

Taking Stock

Stocks are shares of ownership in a corporation. When investors purchase stocks, they are giving the corporation

The New York Stock Exchange

The New York Stock Exchange (NYSE) was opened in 1792. It is located on Wall Street in New York City. There, specialists work to find stock buyers for stock sellers. They make sure that business occurs in a fair and orderly manner. The floor traders stand on the floor of the stock exchange. They wave their hands wildly to show that they want to make trades.

The NYSE includes many companies. The ones who are the best risks for investors are called blue chip companies.

Newspapers and websites often list the performance of companies in the NYSE. Each company has a symbol. For example, General Mills has GIS as its symbol. The listing shows how a company's stock performed on a certain day and its prices: high, low, and at the close of the day. The volume is shown, too, or how many stocks were traded. The range of percentage change up or down is shown. If the stock fell in value, the arrow in the change column points downward. If the stock rose in value the arrow points upward.

The combined performance of all the hundreds of companies is counted, too. A bull market means that the NYSE and other exchanges as a whole are increasing in value. When these markets decrease in value it is known as a bear market.

People pay great attention to the way the NYSE rises and falls. It operates on Monday through Friday from 9:30 am to 4:00 pm Eastern Time.

money that it can use to expand its business. The investors expect to earn money from stocks in two ways. One is dividends. When the company makes a profit, some of this money is paid out as dividends. Often, dividends are paid out *quarterly*, or four times a year. The amount of the dividend can vary depending on how much money the company made.

Did You Know?

Certificates of deposit (CDs) and money market mutual funds are two of the safest investments. Because they are guaranteed by governments and large organizations, investors have little risk of losing their money. However, the return on these investments is not as great as it is for other investments, such as stocks.

If the company does not make a profit in a quarter, it generally does not pay a dividend.

When people believe that a particular company is a good investment, the price of its stock will rise. An investor may decide to sell a stock when the price reaches a certain level. If the investor originally purchased the stock for $30 a share and sells it for $60 a share, she will double her investment, earning a profit of $30 per share. This profit is known as capital gains. But there is also a risk that the stock price will fall if investors are worried about the company's future. An investor who bought stock at $30 a share and sells at $20 a share would lose $10 on each share she purchased.

The New York Stock Exchange (NYSE) is the biggest and most powerful exchange in the US. It sells stocks and bonds. Nasdaq is the National Association of Securities

Dealers Automated Quotation, another market that sells stocks. In Canada, the largest stock exchange is the Toronto Stock Exchange (TSX).

National Economies

Gross Domestic Product (GDP) is a way to measure the health of a country's economy. For each year it includes the total value of all goods and services in a certain country. It does not include those goods and services that were earned by American companies in other countries. The measure that includes that is called the Gross National Product (GNP).

GDP includes financial data from several economic categories. These include national consumption, government spending, and investment. The value of exports are added in as well, but the value of imports are subtracted.

Consumption refers to goods that are supposed to last for more than a few years. It is also food, clothing, and services. Government expenditures are things like roads, schools, and defense. Defense is the military. Investment spending involves business plants and equipment. It also includes family homes. Exports are goods sent out of the country. Imports are goods coming into the country from other places.

The economies of countries are affected by the prices of goods. Inflation increases these prices. When demand for goods outpaces the supply, prices rise sharply. Often, inflation occurs after a war. The government has spent huge amounts on building equipment but has failed to raise enough taxes to pay for it. When inflation is high money falls in value. If, for example, bread was $1.00 a loaf before inflation, but then rises to $2.00, the amount of goods that can be purchased has fallen due to a rise in prices. Inflation usually causes interest rates to rise. Those people on a *fixed income* endure hardships because of it. During times of inflation it is more risky to invest. Deflation is the opposite condition. Prices fall. This tends to occur when employment rises.

Taxes

A tax is a payment that must be made to a local, state/province, or national government. It provides money

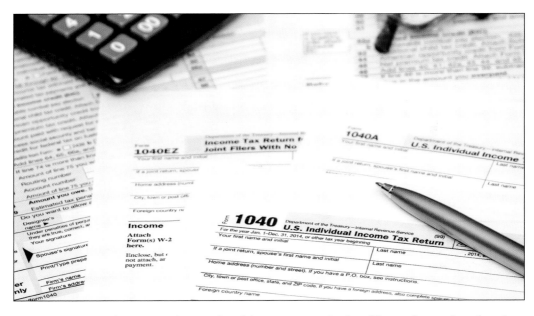

In both the United States and Canada, citizens are required to file tax forms that show how much money they earned in the previous year, and how much they are required to pay in taxes. Tax day is April 15 in the US and April 30 in Canada, although taxpayers are permitted to ask for additional time to file, known as an extension.

to run the governments. Without taxes there would be no police departments, national highways, or local elementary schools.

The national government in the US taxes collects tax on gas, imports, business income, and employees' income. The agency that collects employees' income is called the Internal Revenue Service (IRS). Employers are required to collect money from employees' paychecks and send it to the government. This is supposed to cover most of the employee's tax burden. Each year by April 15, citizens must file a tax return if their income is above a certain level. This level varies according to age and other factors. Taxpayers fill out government forms called tax returns, which show how much they have paid in taxes.

States collect taxes from businesses and sales of goods in their territory. Most states in the US also collect state income tax. They require that a state income tax return be filed. Some states have filers pay a percentage based on their federal income tax. Others use different methods to calculate it.

Government Spending

National governments bring in huge sums from taxes. They also *budget* huge sums to pay for many programs. This includes money for entitlements like Social Security and Medicare. Defense and education also take up large amounts of the government's income. State/province and local governments also spend the taxes they collect. They pay for police, prisons, universities, highways, parks, and more.

 ## Text-Dependent Questions

1. What were two of the oldest forms of money?
2. What elements are used to calculate Gross Domestic Product (GDP)?
3. What is a mortgage?

 ## Research Project

Choose a local, state or province tax such as sales tax or gas tax to research. Locate government figures that identify the percentage or amount of tax collected from individual users. Research what services each tax provides, if any. Find out how much money was collected in total for a recent year. Then create a poster that displays all this information in an attractive manner.

The word specialization *describes focus on a limited number of activities that make products or services more efficient. For instance, a doctor cares for the sick, but he does not know how to repair electronic medical equipment that is not working properly.*

National Economies and Globalization

The free enterprise system operates under the *laissez faire* concept of limited government intervention. However, the government is able to affect the economy if it chooses. The governments of most countries set a fiscal policy that involves spending and *revenue* collection. Annual government spending on areas such as homeland security and education can be huge. The government can raise or lower the amount it spends on these areas. It can also increase taxes or decrease them. These actions affect the country's economy.

Individuals and businesses are affected by changing tax rates. They are also affected by increased growth or decreased demand. In this way the government hopes to keeps the economy more stable.

Monetary policy is related to fiscal policy. It refers to the decisions of central banks. These decisions can keep prices level and help grow jobs. In the US this is done through the Federal Reserve, a system that acts as the country's main bank.

Congress formed it in 1913. It makes sure that the country's banks are healthy. It also helps the economy to be stable. In Canada, monetary policy is watched by the Bank of Canada. Its goal is to keep the currency of Canada strong and to control inflation.

Two Policies

Fiscal and monetary policies are similar, but not the same. They are both tools to change the nation's economy. Monetary policy mainly deals with interest rates. It also oversees the amount of money in *circulation*. The Federal Reserve or Bank of Canada carries out the actions of monetary policy. The government monitors both agencies.

Fiscal policy deals with the levels of spending and taxes. Increasing taxes takes money from the economy because it slows business growth. Lowering taxes drives greater business growth. By spending money the government can also help business grow.

 Words to Understand in This Chapter

circulation—the number of bills and coins existing in the marketplace.
industrialized—having highly developed industry.
revenue—the income collected by a government for public use.
rural—life or people in the country.

The Bank of Canada (in French, Banque du Canada), the nation's central bank under the operation of the government, began operating in 1935. Its mission is "to regulate credit and currency in the best interests of the economic life of the nation."

Economic Advantages

International trade is a large part of the global economy. Each country has special resources. The US grows crops like corn and wheat. Canada produces automobiles. Other areas of the world create different products. Fruit comes from Chile. Electronics from Japan. Oil from the Middle East. Exports and imports are constantly flowing between countries. This is because what one nation lacks another can provide.

Absolute advantage says that one person, group, or nation can produce a good or service at a lower cost than anyone else. It is more efficient than others. For example,

Textile workers sew clothes in a small factory in India. In recent years, many American companies have closed their factories in the United States and moved production to countries in Asia or South America, where the labor costs are lower.

Canada and the United States are both able to produce automobiles. However, if Canada can produce them at better quality and a faster rate than the US it has the absolute advantage. Just because Canada has the absolute advantage does not mean that it should make cars. That is where comparative advantage comes in. It means the production of goods at a lower opportunity cost. By giving a country the ability to sell goods at a lower price, stronger sales result.

An absolute advantage means that a nation is the best at something. A comparative advantage instead involves the costs of an activity. For instance, a woman is a talented artist. She also builds beautiful tables. It takes her a day to paint a picture and a day to build a table. She can sell a picture for $500 and a table for $300. A man across town has the same skills. It takes him two days to paint a picture. He can build a table in three days. His goods sell at the same price.

The woman can make four pictures and three tables in one week for sales of $2,900. The man can make two pictures and one table in a week for sales of $1,300. However, if the woman produces seven pictures in one week she can make $3,500. The man can make 3.5 pictures in one week and earn $1,750. It is to both of their advantages to specialize, or produce only paintings.

Specialization results when a nation produces the best goods using their resources. Because resources are limited, a country must choose to use those resources to produce the goods that are the best value for them.

Trade Between Nations

A trade barrier restricts trade from occurring. One example is a tariff. It is a tax on imported goods, also called customs or duty. It can be used to make a country's goods cheaper than imported goods. This helps the producers of a country's goods.

Another barrier is sanctions. A nation may decide to punish another country for some action. They do this by limiting trade. In the 1960s the United States banned trade and travel to Cuba. The US objected to Cuba's form of gov-

NAFTA

In 1992, the three countries in North America—the United States, Canada, and Mexico—signed a pact called the North American Free Trade Agreement (NAFTA). This agreement eliminated tariffs and other trade barriers among the three countries and created a free-trade bloc, or group of nations joined by agreement. It went into effect on January 1, 1994.

NAFTA was not without its critics, though. US labor unions opposed it. They worried about job losses to companies who would outsource factories to Mexico, where wages would be less expensive. Some protested against NAFTA for environmental reasons. Laws in Mexico offer less protection for the environment than those in Canada and the US.

The economic effects of NAFTA have been positive. US trade with Canada and Mexico makes up the largest export market for more than half of its states. Exports have increased more than 200 percent since its beginning. More than 140,000 small businesses have benefitted as well. Canada reports that since NAFTA went into effect trade has increased almost four times. The development of all three countries created a combined GDP that went from $8 trillion in 1993 to $20 trillion in 2014.

Demonstrators protest against free-trade agreements in Toronto, 2016.

ernment, communism. The US also disagreed with human rights there. Only recently, in 2015, has President Obama eased this sanction.

Trade agreements work to make trade easier between nations. This involves lowering barriers. The World Trade Organization (WTO) works to make trade easier across the globe. It helps to resolve disputes and create agreements.

Two examples of agreements are the European Union and NAFTA. The European Union is a group of countries that agreed to adopt one currency, the Euro. They created a tariff against countries that are not in the union. They also trade as a single market, not individual countries.

The North American Free Trade Agreement, NAFTA, involves the US, Canada, and Mexico. It created a free trade zone between the North American countries. Tariffs have also been eliminated.

Development in the World

Nations across the world differ in many respects, from climate to population. Their economies also differ. Development refers to a process of improvement. A nation that has improved the wellbeing of its citizens is developed. A nation's richness in goods, services, employment and the happiness of its people are measured. Highly developed nations include the United States, Canada, the countries of western Europe, Japan, Australia, and New Zealand. The world's poorest countries are less developed. Afghanistan, Nepal, and Albania are examples.

Countries that are newly *industrialized* are in the

Did You Know?

Not all European countries have joined the European Union. As of 2016 the member countries include: Austria , Belgium, Cyprus, Estonia, Finland, France, Germany, Greece, Ireland, Italy, Latvia, Lithuania, Luxembourg, Malta, The Netherlands, Portugal, Slovakia, Slovenia and Spain.

process of developing. Mexico, Brazil, and eastern Europe are examples.

Every nation faces issues with population growth, health care, and natural resources. The less developed countries usually have more problems than others and less money to deal with these problems. Foreign aid is money that highly developed countries give to less developed ones to help their economies.

International organizations also help with development. Examples are the World Bank, the United Nations, and the International Monetary Fund. They give out loans and help to stabilize economies. Other groups, called nongovernmental organizations (NGOs), also help these economies. They are independent. Some provide food to poor countries. Others, like the Red Cross, focus on relief for natural disasters or wars.

Globalization

The world is interconnected these days. Countries are linked together by financial systems, trade, transportation, and communication. The Internet and technology like cell phones help to make this possible. So do airplane flights that connect the far corners of the earth. This activity

Trainees at the project known as "Connecting 1,500 Women and Girls to the Export Market," in Addis Ababa, Ethiopia. The project trains women and girls to develop skills in industries such as leather, weaving, basketry, embroidery, gemstones, and spinning.

among nations has effects. One is that the free market continues to expand, reaching areas such as the former Soviet Union where communism once ruled. Foreign investors foster trade and inject money into economies of distant lands.

The impact of the Great Recession on the entire world economy was significant. Today, the economies of countries are tied together in such a way that downturns in one nation can and do affect others.

Large corporations often have offices in many countries. These are called multinational corporations. For example, a clothing franchise in the United States may have a factory in Bangladesh where workers sew the clothing. Such operations are profitable for companies because developing nations have lower wages than in the developed world. The act of setting up operations in other countries like this is called outsourcing.

Did You Know?

The Federal Reserve is divided into twelve districts. Each one is located in a different area of the US, the smallest area is located in New York and the largest in the west, including nine states.

Populations are not only growing, they are shifting from place to place. In China, farming has been an age old occupation. Cities, however, give workers chances to make more money and live nearer shopping and entertainment. Because of this, *rural* to urban migration has grown tremendously. The United Nations predicts that 66 percent of the world's population will live in cities by 2050.

Challenges lay ahead for all nations on Earth. Competition for resources remains fierce. The environment must be protected or restored so that future generations have a healthy planet. These and other concerns will cause growth and change in the US, Canada, and across the world. The systems and ideas that govern the study of economics will be in the forefront of those changes.

 ## Text-Dependent Questions

1. What activity is the World Trade Organization involved in?
2. What are the benefits of specialization?
3. What are the differences between absolute advantage and comparative advantage?

 ## Research Project

Choose a developing nation to learn more about. Use library reference books or trusted websites to research funds provided to that country by the World Bank, the United Nations, the International Monetary Fund and at least one non-governmental organizations (NGOs). Create a chart that lists the amounts given for a certain year or period and the reason the amount was provided. Look at the information compiled and write a paragraph that assesses that nation's most pressing economic problems.

Chronology

1776   Adam Smith's book *The Wealth of Nations* sets out the rationale for free market economics.

1792   The New York Stock Exchange (NYSE) is opened; today it is the world's largest stock exchange based on the value of the companies it lists.

1890   The Sherman Anti-Trust Act is passed; this legislation prohibits business activities that will give one company a monopoly over an industry.

1913   The Sixteenth Amendment to the US Constitution allows Congress to levy income taxes; the Federal Reserve System, the central bank of the United States, is created.

1929   In October, the stock market crashes, plunging the United States into the Great Depression.

1935   Legislation is passed that establishes unemployment compensation for American workers who have lost their jobs; The Bank of Canada is established.

1940   The Unemployment Insurance Act is passed in Canada.

1973 The United States experiences a gasoline shortage due to the OPEC oil embargo.

1981 The Canada Post Corporation Act creates a postal monopoly in Canada.

1982 The federal government breaks up the AT&T monopoly.

1984 Canada Health Care Act is passed.

1994 The North American Free Trade Agreement (NAFTA) eliminates tariffs on most trade between Canada, Mexico, and the United States.

This statue of a charging bull in the financial district of Lower Manhattan represents aggressive financial optimism and prosperity.

1996 In the United States, housing prices begin to boom, rising by an average of 10 percent a year.

1999 The federal government wins an antitrust suit against Microsoft, requiring the company to open its software so that other web browsers will work properly on Windows-based personal computers.

2006 Housing prices reach their peak; homeowners begin to default on subprime mortgages that they cannot afford to pay.

2007 The failure of several major financial institutions and the collapse of the housing bubble leads to the start of the Great Recession.

2008 The government passes the Troubled Asset Relief Program (TARP) to bail out major companies in danger of closing.

2016 In February the United States and other Pacific Rim countries sign the Trans-Pacific Partnership, a free-trade agreement.

Organizations to Contact

Bank of Canada
234 Laurier Avenue West
Ottawa, Ontario
K1A 0G9
Canada
Phone: 1.800.303.1282
Fax: 613.782.7713
Email: info@bankofcanada.ca
Website: http://www.bankofcanada.ca/

Federal Reserve
Constitution Ave NW & 20th St NW
Washington, DC
Phone: 888-851-1920
Website: http://www.federalreserve.gov/

New York Stock Exchange (NYSE)
11 Wall Street
New York, NY 10005
Phone: (212) 656-3000
Website: http://www.nyse.com/

Organisation for Economic Co-operation and Development (OECD)
Washington Centre
2001 L Street, NW, Suite 650,
Washington, DC 20036-4922
Phone: (202) 785-6323
Fax: (202) 785-0350
E-mail: washington.contact@oecd.org
Website: www.oecd.org

Toronto Stock Exchange (TSX)
The Exchange Tower
130 King Street West
Toronto, ON
M5X 1J2
Canada
Phone: +1 888 873-8392
Fax: +1 416 947-4662
Email: info@tmx.com
Website: http://www.tmx.com/

US Chamber of Commerce
1615 H Street, NW
Washington, DC 20062
Phone: (202) 659-6000
Fax: (202) 463-3126
Email: Americas@uschamber.com
Website: www.uschamber.com

World Trade Organization (WTO)
Centre William Rappard
Rue de Lausanne 154
CH-1211 Geneva 21
Switzerland
Phone: +41 (0)22 739-5111
Fax: +41 (0)22 731-4206
Email: enquiries@wto.org
Website: www.wto.org

Series Glossary

barter—the official department that administers and collects the duties levied by a government on imported goods.

bond—a debt investment used by companies and national, state, or local governments to raise money to finance projects and activities. The corporation or government borrows money for a defined period of time at a variable or fixed interest rate.

credit—the ability of a customer to obtain goods or services before payment, based on the trust that payment will be made in the future.

customs—the official department that administers and collects the duties or tariffs levied by a government on imported goods.

debt—money, or something else, that is owed or due in exchange for goods or services.

demurrage—extra charges paid to a ship or aircraft owner when a specified period for loading or unloading freight has been exceeded.

distributor—a wholesaler or middleman engaged in the distribution of a category of goods, esp to retailers in a specific area.

duty—a tax on imported goods.

export—to send goods or services to another country for sale.

Federal Reserve—the central bank of the United States, which controls the amount of money circulating in the US economy and helps to set interest rates for commercial banks.

import—to bring goods or services into a country from abroad for sale.

interest—a fee that is paid in exchange for the use of money that has been borrowed, or for delaying the repayment of a debt.

stock—an ownership interest in a company. Stocks are sold by companies to raise money for their operations. The price of a successful company's stock will typically rise, which means the person who originally bought the stock can sell it and earn a profit.

tariff—a government-imposed tax that must be paid on certain imported or exported goods.

value added tax (VAT)—a type of consumption tax that is placed on a product whenever value is added at each stage of production and at final sale. VAT is often used in the European Union.

World Bank—an international financial organization, connected to the United Nations. It is the largest source of financial aid to developing countries.

Further Reading

Cohn, Jessica. *What is Scarcity of Resources?* St. Catharines, Ont.: Crabtree Publishing, 2008.

Crayton, Lisa. *Globalization: What It Is and How It Works.* New York: Enslow, 2016.

Larson, Jennifer S. *Who's Buying? Who's Selling?: Understanding Consumers and Producers: Exploring Economics.* Minneapolis: Lerner Classroom, 2010.

Matthews, Sheelagh. *Trade and Global Impact.* Calgary, Alberta, Canada: Weigl, 2010.

Prados, Elena Fernandez. *Economics through Everyday Stories from around the World.* New York: CreateSpace, 2016.

Schwartz, Heather. *Goods and Services Around Town.* Huntington Beach, Calif.: Teacher Created Materials, 2013.

Internet Resources

www.cia.gov/library/publications/resources/the-world-factbook
The CIA World Factbook provides a wealth of information about every country in the world, including a detailed section on each country's economy.

www.jamyway.org
Young people learn about money, businesses, and more in a colorful, easy-to-digest format.

www.frbsf.org/education/teacher-resources/american-currency-exhibit
The Federal Reserve Bank of San Francisco provides online galleries of American Currency, which provides information about money in US history.

http://teacher.scholastic.com/scholasticnews/games_quizzes/economics/
Word Scrambles and quizzes that make learning about economics fun.

www.scholastic.com/browse/article.jsp?id = 3750497
Scholastic Magazine issues this special article for kids detailing the global economic crisis that became known at the Great Recession.

Index

absolute advantage, 49–51
Affordable Care Act, 23
American Recovery and
    Reinvestment Act, 12
antitrust laws, 33

Bank of Canada, 12, 48, **49**
banks, 7, 9–10, 38–39, **49**
    Federal Reserve, 47–48, 54
    in the Great Recession, 10–11,
        12, 13
barriers to market entry, 32, 33
    See also markets
bonds, 39
    See also investments
boom and bust cycles, 6–8, 9–13
    See also economics
business types, 34–35
Butz, Jennifer, 5

Canada, 10, 11–13, 24, 29–30, 41, 48,
    49
    and Canada Post, 34
    health care in, 23
    and NAFTA, 52, 53
Canada Post Corporation Act, 34
capitalism, 22–23
    See also free market economies
centrally planned economy. *See* command economies
certificates of deposit, 39, 41
    See also investments
China, **21**, 22, **24**, 25

command economies, 20–22
commodities, 32
communism, **20, 21**, 22, 25
comparative advantage, 50
corporate bonds, 39
currency, **36**, 37
    See also money

deflation, 43
demand. *See* supply and demand,
    law of
depressions, 6, 8, 9–10
disequilibrium, 28
Dodd-Frank Wall Street Reform and
    Consumer Protection Act (Dodd-
    Frank Act), 12
downturns, economic, 6–7, 9–13

economic system, 18
economics
    boom and bust cycles in, 6–8,
        9–13
    and business types, 34–35
    and development of countries, 53
    and fiscal policy, 47, 48
    and international trade, **14**,
        48–53, 54–55
    and the law of supply and
        demand, **26,** 27–34
    and market types, 31–32
    and monetary policy, 47–48
    and monopolies, 33–34
    and opportunity costs, 16–17

Numbers in ***bold italic*** refer to captions.

and pricing, *26*, 27–29, 30–31, 33, 43
and scarcity, 15–16
in a society, 18
and types of economies, 18–25, 47
See also money
elasticity of demand, 30–31
See also supply and demand, law of
Employment Insurance, 12
equilibrium, 28–29
European Union, 51, 53

Federal Reserve, 47–48, 54
fiscal policy, 47, 48
free market economies, 22–24, 47

globalization, *14*, 54–55
and international trade, 48–53
government, 28–29, 33, 45
and fiscal policy, 47
and the Great Recession, 10–11, 12
laissez faire, 20, 24, 47
Great Depression, 9–10, *11*
Great Recession, 5–6, *7*, 8–9, 10–13, 54
gross domestic product (GDP), *40*, 43, 52
gross national product (GNP), 43

health care, 23
housing bubble, 8–9

inflation, 43
interest rates, 10, 12
international trade, 48–53
and globalization, *14*, 54–55
investments, 6, 9, 38–39, 41

laissez-faire government, 20, 24, 47
law of supply and demand. *See* supply and
demand, law of

Mao Zedong, *21*
markets, 31–32, 33
Marx, Karl, *20*
Microsoft, 34
minimum wages, 29–30
mixed economies, 25
monetary policy, 47–48
money
bonds, 39

characteristics of, 37–38
and currency, *36*, 37–38
and inflation, 43
and investments, 6, 9, 38–39, 41
and taxes, 43–45, 47, 48
See also economics
money market mutual funds, 39, 41
See also investments
monopolies, 33–34
municipal bonds, 39

Nasdaq, 41
natural monopoly, 33–34
New York Stock Exchange, *4*, 41, 42
See also stock market
nongovernmental organizations (NGOs),
53
North American Free Trade Agreement
(NAFTA), 51, 52, 53

Obama, Barack, 12
oil, *31*, 33
opportunity costs, 16–17
Organization of Petroleum Exporting
Countries (OPEC), 3

partnerships, 35
perfect competition, 31–32
pricing, *26*, 27–29, 30–31, 33, 43

recessions, 5–9, 10–13, 54
rent control, 28–29
research projects, 13, 25, 35, 45, 55

sanctions, 51
Sankey, Laura, 6
savings bonds, 39
scarcity, 15–16
Sherman Anti-Trust Act, 33
Smith, Adam, 22–23
socialism, 20, 22, 23
sole proprietorships, 34–35
specialization, *46*, 51
stock market, *4*, 9–10, 35, 41–42
supply and demand, law of, *26*, 27, 29–30
and competition, 31–32
and elasticity of demand, 30–31
and monopolies, 33–34

and pricing, 27–29, 30–31
See also economics
Sutton, David, 5–6

tariffs, 51, 52, 53
taxes, 43–45, 47, 48
trade agreements, 51–53
trade barriers, 51, 52
traditional economies, 18–19
treasury bonds, 39
Troubled Asset Relief Program (TARP),
  12

unemployment, *8*, 10, 11–12

The Wealth of Nations (Smith), 22–23
World Trade Organization (WTO), 51

About the Author

Xina M. Uhl discovered her love of social studies while still in grade school. She went on to obtain a Master of Arts in history from California State University, Northridge. After teaching college-level history she moved into educational writing. She has authored books, textbooks, teacher's guides, lessons, and assessment questions. When she is not writing she enjoys travel, photography, and hiking with her dogs. Her blog features her travel adventures and latest fiction projects at http://xuwriter.wordpress.com. She makes her home in sunny Southern California with her family.